THE
COLLEGE
BOUND
PLANNER

For All Students Planning to Apply to College

THE
COLLEGE
BOUND
PLANNER

A Roadmap to Take You from High School to Your First Day of College

ANNA COSTARAS & GAIL LISS

mango
PUBLISHING

CORAL GABLES

Cover Design: Roberto Núñez
Cover Illustration: ~ Bitter ~/AdobeStock
Layout & Design: Megan Werner

For permission requests, please contact the publisher at:
Mango Publishing Group
2850 S Douglas Road, 2nd Floor
Coral Gables, FL 33134 USA
info@mango.bz

For special orders, quantity sales, course adoptions and corporate sales, please email the publisher at sales@mango.bz. For trade and wholesale sales, please contact Ingram Publisher Services at customer.service@ingramcontent.com or +1.800.509.4887.

The College Bound Planner: A Roadmap to Take You From High School to Your First Day of College

Library of Congress Cataloging-in-Publication number: 2021938726
ISBN: (print) 978-1-64250-604-4, (ebook) 978-1-64250-605-1
BISAC category code STU009000, STUDY AIDS / College Entrance

Printed in the United States of America

TABLE OF CONTENTS

INTRODUCTION

Your goal is to go to college, and for that, you will need to be college ready. Picture yourself in senior year, you'll want to have choices about where to apply and where to attend. Engage in a bit of self-discovery in order to get yourself on the right path. Find out what you enjoy, what you're good at and what challenges you. What you achieve in high school and beyond is all up to you.

High school is the time to start imagining the possibilities. These are four years to use for self-exploration, growing as a student, becoming more comfortable socially, maturing and gaining greater independence. So take control—become accountable for your actions and work hard to become the best version of yourself. Nurture your curiosity and learn about the world around you. You'll be more aware, as well as a more interesting person.

Becoming your best self is a process and ninth grade is just the start. The sooner you understand how the decisions you make throughout high school affect your college options, the better you can plan for your future. Pick up this book any time in high school. It's never too early or too late to begin. Read through the entire book to get a preview of what's ahead and to make the most of your college bound journey.

We will help you:

- ► Find the academic direction and extracurricular activities that allow you to grow.

- ► Develop good study skills and life habits to set yourself up to succeed.

- ► Get organized and stay organized.

- ► Know what you should be doing at any time in high school.

- ► Answer the question, "How do I see myself?" to effectively tell admissions who you are and what you will bring to their campus.

- ► Understand the application process and successfully apply.

- ► Get ready for the first day as an undergraduate.

Let's work together to create your roadmap to college.

Anna and Gail

CHAPTER 1

FRESHMAN YEAR: ON YOUR MARK, GET SET, GO

T his school year will begin with so many new things: school supplies, books, classmates, classes, teachers and even possibly your school. This is an opportunity for a fresh start, a chance for a reset, to position yourself where you want to be.

High school is the next step in your academic journey and you'll find school will be different now than what you've been used to. The building might be bigger and it may take you some time to find your way around. Your class may be larger, with many unfamiliar faces and new friends to make. But the most significant difference will most certainly be your workload. Now that you're in high school, you should anticipate being challenged with more complex academic material, while at the same time you'll be expected to be more independent. Your full-time responsibility is to be a committed student.

Although this may sound daunting, it is important to keep in mind that starting in freshman year, everything you do will impact your college options. Begin by asking yourself, "Who am I?" Although this question may seem simple, it's not so easy to answer. Who you are and how you'll present yourself to colleges will be reflected through your curriculum, your grades, how hard you push yourself academically and your involvement in extracurricular and community activities. For success in college, you will need to become prepared by completing the necessary academic coursework. You have four years to become college ready, but don't worry, no one expects you to have it all figured out on day one. You'll have time and plenty of help.

A good support system is so important. Build your team and include your parents, after all, they know you best. Your guidance counselor, teachers, school psychologist, peer mentors and even your school principal could all be members of your team and may have much to offer. Introduce yourself and take the time to build these relationships. Don't be shy, keep your group in the loop and ask for support. Be proactive and reach out for help when you're feeling uncertain or overwhelmed.

Now that you're in ninth grade, set some personal and academic goals. Be engaged and present in your classes. Your job is to take your studies seriously. Come to school every day on time and prepared to learn, and use your time in high school to set yourself up for college. Participate, speak up, share your thoughts and ask questions when you're not clear about the material.

You should have some fun and enjoy yourself too. Explore life outside of the classroom. Jump into activities you know you like or try something you haven't done before. You'll develop new interests and skills, and show colleges how you spent your time. They will be interested to see what you did outside the classroom and how you contributed to your school and local community.

Students and parents want to know what it takes to get into a "good" college. There's no single magic answer. The answer depends on the student, their goals, the type of school they'd like to attend, and each college's admissions criteria and objectives, which may vary from year to year. College admissions reps want to see that you have used your four years in high school to challenge yourself, develop academically and grow personally.

GAME PLAN

Set Your Goals

What It Means to
Be "College Ready"

Meet Your
Guidance Counselor

Get Involved

Set Yourself Up
to Succeed

Set Your Goals

Goal setting is an important skill to develop and one that will help you in high school, college and from then on. Studies have shown that when you write down and share your goals, you are more likely to stick with them. Seeing them visually helps you stay committed, so make your list and then share it with someone close to you.

Use the prompts below to help you start thinking about who you are, what you care about, where you're headed and how you're going to get there. You may have very specific responses to some questions, while you may not be sure about others—that's natural. Talk to your family to get feedback and hear what they think.

Once you've gathered your thoughts, share them with your guidance counselor.

DEFINE YOUR STRENGTHS

The natural place to start when looking for classes is by identifying your academic interests and strengths. For example, if you excel in math, talk to your counselor about enrolling in the most challenging level you are eligible for now. Find out which prerequisites you are required to take to be able to enroll in the more advanced classes later in high school.

What do you do well?

_____

_____

_____

_____

What interests you?

_____

_____

_____

_____

Are there any particular courses that you'd like to explore?

_____

_____

_____

_____

What comes easily to you?

_____

_____

_____

What accomplishments are you most proud of?

_____

_____

_____

_____

Use these prompts to help you narrow down the large selection of courses available at your school.

Classes I'd Like to Take

✏ IDENTIFY WHAT YOU NEED TO WORK ON

Start off ninth grade by figuring out what you need help with. Maybe you just need a boost in your comfort level with a particular subject. For example, if you're having difficulty starting your writing assignments, sign up for a writing workshop. In the past, if you have found new math concepts frustrating at first, get a jump start and attend extra help sessions so you don't fall behind.

What do you wish you could do better?

_____

_____

_____

_____

Name something new you'd like to learn.

_____

_____

_____

_____

What makes you uncomfortable?

_____

_____

_____

_____

_____

When do you find yourself procrastinating?

_____

_____

_____

_____

_____

Talk about your responses with your guidance counselor to
get help identifying classes, seminars and extra help or practice
that would improve your skills and boost your confidence.

Things I Need Help With

_____

_____

_____

_____

_____

_____

_____

THINK ABOUT WHERE YOU WANT TO BE IN FOUR YEARS

Now that you're in high school, you'll start hearing other students talk about college. Keep your ears open and go back to your guidance counselor with your questions to get the real scoop, since there is so much misinformation circulating. While you may not know what type of school you'll ultimately be interested in, this is the time to start thinking about what appeals to you.

Are there any schools you've dreamed of attending?

_____

_____

_____

_____

_____

Is there a type of school you see yourself attending (city or rural, large or small)?

_____

_____

_____

_____

_____

Is there a subject you'd like to study in college?

_____

_____

_____

_____

Is there a field in which you hope to work?

_____

_____

_____

_____

66

I couldn't sign up for AP physics in senior year because I hadn't completed all the science prerequisites. I wish I had known from the start of high school so I could have planned better.

—Nicole M.

99

DEFINE YOUR PERSONAL GOALS

Think about what you'd like to achieve in the next four years. High school is about more than just going to class and completing your homework. This is the time to explore and learn more about yourself, your interests and the opportunities available to you. For example, do you have the ability to be a recruited athlete or is it more realistic for you to join the intramural team? Do you aspire to be president of your class? If you want to perform with the theater group, this is the time to try. You may decide to follow an interest during high school simply because it's something you enjoy or you may be hoping to continue your involvement in college and even beyond.

Is there a skill that you'd like to improve?

_____

_____

_____

_____

_____

Do you have a particular passion you'd like to pursue?

_____

_____

_____

_____

Are there any new interests you'd like to learn more about?

_____

_____

_____

_____

What It Means to Be "College Ready"

"College Ready" means having the academic preparedness you'll need to begin college. It means you will have mastered skills including note taking, studying, test taking and writing essays and research papers. Being college ready is also about having life skills such as time management, critical thinking, problem solving, decision making and communication, as well as the discipline and drive needed to succeed.

Work hard in high school and challenge yourself so you will be ready for the rigor of college courses. Your goal in high school is to become college ready and to be able to demonstrate this to college admissions when it's time for you to apply.

College may seem far away, but thinking ahead and understanding how things work will help you prepare. The college admissions assessment process is a multistep one. Most schools approach admissions "holistically," meaning they consider the candidate as a whole and not just the empirical data. Traditionally, grades and test scores have been the first hurdle to cross in order to be considered, as admissions officers believed high school grades to be the best indicator of future college academic performance.

All students will need to be college ready, regardless of the type of college or university they hope to attend. You should plan to take the most rigorous courses available to you to help you grow academically. Your transcript will list your courses, so colleges will see how you chose to challenge yourself. If your goal is to attend a highly competitive university, strive to take the most advanced classes offered by your high school in subjects in which you excel and find interesting. For example, if your school offers numerous Advanced Placement (AP) classes and you haven't taken any by the time you apply to college, you will not have demonstrated that you challenged yourself. If your high school does not offer any APs, yet you have taken honors classes, you will have shown a high level of academic motivation. Applying yourself now is going to impact where you head next.

Schools will assess your readiness by reviewing the following:

▶ The rigor of your high school curriculum
▶ The grades you earned in challenging classes, which should reflect positively on your overall academic profile

- ► The grades you earned in all your classes and whether your grades have been consistent, improved, or declined over the four years

- ► Your standardized test scores, if required and/ or submitted

And while we're on the subject of academic performance...

Did you know that your grades will not only be considered for admission, but may also help you to qualify for merit aid? Merit aid is not dependent on financial need and does not have to be repaid.

- ► Once you've met their academic criteria, colleges will consider the following soft factors:

- ► Extracurricular activities and community involvement to help them to get an idea of what you have contributed to your high school and local communities, so they can gauge what you'll bring to their community

- ▶ The personal essay(s) you write for your college applications to convey who you are beyond your grades and test scores

- ▶ Any special talent you may have

- ▶ Letters of recommendation from your teachers, counselor, a coach, mentor, or special program director

- ▶ Whether you have demonstrated interest in attending their school

66

I wish I knew what a college application looked like. I would have gotten more involved in school and had more to write about.

—Juan A.

99

Meet Your Guidance Counselor

Your guidance counselor can be your most valuable resource. First, your counselor knows what your high school has to offer and how to help you to get the most out of your four years there. Second, they understand the college process and what colleges are looking for. It's imperative that your counselor get to know you early on to help you map out your personalized plan to reach your goal of being college ready. This is a fluid process that needs to be adjusted as you make your way through high school. Meet each year to check in, review your progress, plan ahead for your following year and make sure you're on track.

Becoming college ready is not only about course selection and grades. It's about maximizing your potential as a student and as a contributing member of your community. It's about developing and exploring interests and identifying where you excel. High school is a time for personal growth. Again, this is where your counselor comes in. If your counselor knows you, then they'll keep you in mind when they hear of opportunities that fit your particular interests and objectives. They'll also know of programs in your community that match your interests and can suggest ways to volunteer and spend the summer.

Your counselor will help you to understand your school's grading system, your state's testing and graduation requirements, and the types of diplomas and distinctions you can graduate with. Criteria to qualify for honors societies vary from school to school, so your counselor can explain details if you're hoping to be inducted. If you're an athlete, learn about NCAA eligibility requirements from your counselor.

Meet early in ninth grade to cover the following:

DEFINE YOUR ACADEMIC GOALS

Do you want to apply to a pre-med program? Do you want to attend an art school? Are you interested in computer science? Outlining your objectives early on will allow you to choose the appropriate academic track to help you get there. Learn about your school's course offerings, how you'll be placed and how much choice you have in the classes you'll be registering for going forward. For example, if your goal is to qualify for AP classes, you'll need to know the prerequisites and complete them before registering.

If you don't know what you'd like to study in
college, don't worry. Most high school students do
not, so in addition to all the required classes, take a
variety of electives to explore the possibilities.

 Filling in the following prompts and discussing your responses
with your counselor will help to provide some direction for
your conversation about course selection.

What is your favorite subject?

_____

_____

_____

_____

What is your strongest subject?

_____

_____

_____

_____

Would you like to improve your performance in any particular subject(s)?

_____

_____

_____

_____

_____

What new areas do you think you'd like to try?

_____

_____

_____

_____

_____

Courses to Keep in Mind for Next Year

 SHARE YOUR INDIVIDUAL NEEDS OR CIRCUMSTANCES

You may need a quiet space to study after school, academic support such as tutoring or additional time for testing. Your guidance counselor is the one who can set up special testing accommodations. They can also direct you on how to arrange for extra help. Maybe you need to sign up for reduced or free meals at school and don't know how to apply. Perhaps there's something going on at home that you're having trouble dealing with. Talk to your guidance counselor, they can either offer support or direct you to someone who can. Don't be shy, remember to speak up as soon as you're struggling. Now that you're in high school, you need to advocate for yourself.

66

If I had gone to the math lab for extra help, I wouldn't have fallen behind. I spent the second half of the year trying to catch up and improve my average.

—Emily S.   99

Get Involved

High school is about growing and becoming your own person. This is the time to try new things in order to give yourself experiences that will enable you to learn more about yourself. Finding activities you like will help you figure out what you enjoy and what you're good at doing, as well as giving you a chance to develop new skills such as leadership, public speaking and teamwork. Your activities may even point you toward future opportunities and will give you something to share with college admissions reps. It's easiest to gravitate toward things that come easily to you, but try to step out of your comfort zone and make an effort to join something new. The more you try, the more you'll find out about yourself and what you like to do.

College admissions reps will be interested in understanding who you are as an individual beyond your academic accomplishments and they will want to know what you really care about. Now is the time to explore clubs and activities so you can identify what interests you and what to get involved in.

SELF-EXPLORATION
TOP 10 QUESTIONS TO ASK YOURSELF

1. **Do you like to write?**

   If you do, join your school's newspaper, yearbook or literary magazine.

2. **Are you athletic?**

   If you are, try out for varsity, junior varsity, intramural, police athletic league (PAL), travel teams or junior USTA.

3. **Are you interested in theatre?**

   If so, try out for the school play, help out with set, lighting, or sound design or join a community theatre or dance group.

4. **Do you play a musical instrument?**

   If you do, join your school's orchestra, marching band, concert band or jazz band.

5. **Do you like to read?**

   If the answer is yes, join a book club.

6. **Are you interested in the business world?**

   If so, join the Future Business Leaders of America or a similar investment club.

7. **Are you interested in volunteering?**

   If yes, help out with Habitat for Humanity, at a local soup kitchen or as an after-school tutor.

8. **Do you want to challenge yourself by joining an academic club?**

   If you do, participate in science research, mathletes, the Rube Goldberg Machine Contest, chess club or a foreign language club.

9. **Are you creative?**

   If you are, express yourself by joining the photography club or maybe helping with set design.

10. **Are you interested in public speaking?**

   If so, join the debate club or mock trial team.

If your school hosts an activities fair, make sure to attend. This is a chance to get information about what each club does, how often they meet and how many members participate. This should help you home in on the clubs and activities you'd like to join so you can get started.

Top Clubs to Learn More About

Set Yourself Up to Succeed

When you were in middle school, your teachers and parents were most likely managing your time and progress. This responsibility is now yours, so you need to establish good routines, both academically and personally. These habits will help you balance your responsibilities in high school and prepare you to be a college student.

GET INTO GOOD STUDY HABITS

Now that you're in high school, you are going to be held to a different standard. You will be expected to work independently, manage your assignments and turn your work in on time. Recognize that high school can be very demanding and that every grade counts. Developing good study habits early on will help put you on the path to academic success.

✓ Begin by finding a good spot to study, whether in your home, at your school or in the public library, and make sure this is a place with few distractions.

✓ Always remember to turn off your phone so you don't get distracted.

✓ Pace yourself. Don't underestimate how long each assignment will take to complete.

✓ Make yourself a timeline to help keep up with school work and meet deadlines.

✓ Form a study group or find a study partner to review with before your tests.

✓ Ask for help if you find yourself falling behind or having difficulty with a topic. Most teachers offer extra help sessions and many schools offer peer tutoring.

And while we're on the subject of good study habits...

Did you know that being distracted by technology has been proven to negatively impact school performance? Doing homework while dividing your attention means assignments will take longer to complete, you're more apt to make mistakes and your retention of material will be impaired. So turn off your phones and tablets while doing homework and studying to avoid distractions.

IMPLEMENT POSITIVE ROUTINES

How you manage your personal time affects how you do in school. Figure out what it takes for you to be at the top of your game. There are no rules here; the important thing is to find out what works best for you.

✓ Be on time for school. If being rushed makes you feel stressed, leave yourself enough time to get ready at your own pace.

✓ Get enough sleep so you can be at your best. Studies have found that sleep benefits the brain and promotes attention, memory, and analytical thought.

✓ Balance your schedule. It's so important to leave yourself time away from school and studies to just have some fun.

✓ Evaluate your commitments. If you feel overstressed and your grades are suffering, then consider cutting back on activities.

66

My family had a tech-free dinner rule. At first, I resisted. After a few nights, I realized it was nice to have a little time off-line and talk together.

—Jack V.   99

☑ GET ORGANIZED

Now that you're in high school, you'll find you have many more demands on your time as you juggle schoolwork, extracurriculars, family and friends. It's up to you to set priorities and budget your time accordingly. Being organized will help you be successful and meet your goals throughout high school.

✓ Keep a planner or calendar. Time management means keeping track of due dates and estimating how much time you'll need to prepare for tests and complete assignments. Enter these dates in your calendar to make sure to leave yourself enough time to prepare.

✓ Keep track of appointments. Enter the date and time you've scheduled to meet with your guidance counselor or advisor, club meetings, tryout dates and your work schedule, to name a few.

✓ Check your planner daily to stay on top of things.

✓ Establish a filing system for your schoolwork, including your notes, quizzes and teacher handouts to make studying for exams easier and more effective.

✓ Create a college folder on your computer or store a paper version in a safe place. You'll use this folder throughout high school to collect important documents including schoolwork, lists of passwords and other information that you will need for your college applications.

✓ Create a list of your extracurricular activities, including clubs, athletics, community service, as well as work and summer experiences. Keep track of how much time you spend per week on each activity and list any positions you hold, beginning in ninth grade. Also, list awards you earn and competitions in which you participate. Keep this list up-to-date, as you'll need this information when the time comes to fill out your applications because it will be hard to remember all the details looking back later.

Try This

☺ Know where help is available at your school and where to find it.

☺ Figure out and pursue what you're genuinely interested in.

☺ Get into the habit of reading the newspaper, whether online or in print; you'll be informed, you'll become a better writer, have more to say and improve your vocabulary.

☺ Sign up for the word of the day (with College Board or Word Genius). It takes a long time to build a good vocabulary.

Goals

- [ ] _____
- [ ] _____
- [ ] _____
- [ ] _____
- [ ] _____
- [ ] _____
- [ ] _____
- [ ] _____
- [ ] _____
- [ ] _____
- [ ] _____
- [ ] _____
- [ ] _____
- [ ] _____

☐ _____

☐ _____

☐ _____

☐ _____

☐ _____

☐ _____

☐ _____

☐ _____

☐ _____

☐ _____

☐ _____

☐ _____

☐ _____

☐ _____

☐ _____

☐ _____

☐ _____

Notes

CHAPTER 2

SOPHOMORE YEAR: DIVE IN

While freshman year was exciting and full of new experiences, you can expect to feel more settled and comfortable in sophomore year. This is a time to continue to find your way and identify what works for you. Looking back, are you happy with your academic performance so far? Would you have done anything differently? Did you leave yourself time to have some fun too? As hard as you may be working on your schoolwork, find time to devote to activities outside the classroom that you enjoy.

As a sophomore, you still have plenty of time to change things, so don't miss out on this opportunity to reset your strategy if that makes sense for you. It's early enough in high school to implement a new plan. Make sure to challenge yourself; you'll get more out of high school. Remember your job is to work hard and be a dedicated student.

Build on your relationship with your guidance counselor. Schedule a meeting to review what you've done so far and what you hope to achieve this school year. Ask for input on whether you're on the right path. Begin talking about your standardized test options. This is also the time to address any personal concerns. Let your counselor help you so you can start the school year on a positive note. Continue to develop a rapport with your teachers. Your teachers are an important part of your support system. The better they know you, the more effective they can be in offering you extra help or even additional enrichment in their subject.

Do you have a good routine—one that worked for you throughout ninth grade? Or did your schedule leave you feeling stressed and stretched in too many directions with little down time for yourself? If you feel like your routine didn't work, figure out why. Were you involved in too many extracurriculars? Consider focusing on only a few of your favorites to open up your schedule. Did you have enough time to complete your assignments and study for exams? If the answer is no, allocate more time by starting your work sooner.

Focus on being organized. Remember to set up a calendar for the new school year and fill in all your deadlines for assignments and tests, along with any appointments. Also, mark your calendar to help you keep track of after-school events such as club meetings or volunteer commitments. Get organized from the start, and you'll be more in control and avoid unnecessary mistakes and stress. Make sure your schoolwork throughout the semester is saved in a way that makes it easy to go through the material when it's time to study for exams. If your system is not working and you need some new ideas, talk to your guidance counselor, teachers, parents, siblings and maybe even a mentor for suggestions.

> I got off to a slow start in freshman year. I'm so glad I took my guidance counselor's suggestion and signed up for the study skills workshop offered at the beginning of sophomore year.
>
> —Sam K.

VOCABULARY WORDS

STANDARDIZED TESTS

ACT: This standardized test is administered by ACT and used for college admissions. The total score is between 1 and 36, testing English, math, reading, and science. Go to www.act.org to register.

ADVANCED PLACEMENT (AP): These tests are given by the College Board and are offered at the end of the corresponding class. Depending on the college or university and the test score you earn on each AP test, you may be awarded college credit. You may also be able to skip a prerequisite course or two, such as basic freshman English, if you score well on that exam.

NATIONAL MERIT SCHOLARSHIP PROGRAM: The National Merit Scholarship Program is an annual competition for high school students planning to attend college. Students need to take the PSAT/NMSQT, in their junior year and earn a top score to be eligible for scholarships and recognition through the program.

PRE-ACT: A practice ACT, this exam offered in tenth grade helps students identify areas for improvement. Total score is between 1 and 36 with the following subsections: English, math, reading, and science.

PSAT/NMSQT: The Preliminary SAT/National Merit Scholarship Qualifying Test is a standardized test administered by the College Board and cosponsored by the National Merit Scholarship Corporation. The PSAT is a multiple-choice practice exam for the SAT that tests reading and math skills. The test is offered in tenth or eleventh grade.

SAT: The SAT is a multiple-choice standardized test administered by the College Board that is used for college admissions. Registration information can be found on: www.collegereadiness.collegeboard.org/sat/register. The test has two sections: Math and Evidence-Based Reading, with a total score range of 400 to 1600.

SCORE CHOICE: Score choice allows students to submit their highest section scores from their SAT or ACT tests across multiple test dates to prospective colleges. Some, but not all colleges and universities use score choice, aslo known as super scoring.

TEST BLIND: A college admissions policy that does not require students to submit standardized test scores with their college applications.

TEST OPTIONAL: An admissions policy in which it is not mandatory to submit standardized scores. However, scores are considered if submitted.

GAME PLAN

Do Your "Job"

A First Look At
Standardized Tests

Build on
Your Credentials

Be Organized

Plan Ahead

Do Your "Job"

Your full-time job is to be a student. Do your job well by being the best student you can be. This is a new school year and you know your way around now. You know what you need to do, so jump right in. Stay focused and work hard so you don't fall behind. Your grades are the best indicator of how well you're doing your "job" and will be the first thing that college admissions reps will review. Put your best effort into each assignment and every test as it's very difficult to turn things around once you average in one disappointing grade.

66

You don't want to look back and say, 'I should have worked harder.'

—Bill P.

99

➤ Speak with your guidance counselor

If you are not satisfied with your academic performance so far, you need to identify why you were unable to achieve your goals. Your counselor may have some suggestions on how to turn things around.

➤ Meet with your teachers

As classes begin, introduce yourself to your teachers and get a clear understanding of their expectations. Ask how you will be graded and how much weight will be given to your performance on quizzes, tests, papers and class participation. Take advantage of teacher-led extra help sessions. This is where you can ask questions, build on your mastery of the subject matter, practice and further develop your skills, and get to know your teachers better.

➤ Keep up the good work

If things are going well, think about stepping it up. You may want to consider new ways to challenge yourself. Sign up for competitions, pursue research projects, join mathletes, write for the school paper or volunteer to be a peer tutor.

Don't wait for your counselor to reach out to you, be proactive and schedule appointments to meet throughout the school year.

—Samir T.

A First Look at Standardized Tests

Start a conversation about testing with your guidance counselor. Although it may seem a little early to be doing this, there are some choices about standardized testing you will be making this year.

✓ **Find out about your school's PSAT sign-up process.** The test is typically given at school in October of either tenth or eleventh grade, so confirm the test date with your guidance office.

✓ **Look at an online PSAT on the College Board's website** so you know what to expect on test day.

✓ **Review your results with your counselor** and identify your strengths and weaknesses. If you take the test in tenth grade and have a shot at a merit scholarship, talk about how to best prepare to retake the test in junior year.

✓ **Sort through the mail and emails** you'll receive from colleges and universities. If you opted in to be contacted, you will be targeted by a variety of schools based on your demographics, test scores and the career interests you indicated when you registered.

✓ **Talk about how AP courses fit into your academic plan** for junior and senior years. If you're enrolled in APs this year, you'll register during the spring for the exam(s). Tests are given in school at the end of the second semester.

And while we're on the subject of Advanced Placement classes...

Did you know that if a college accepts your AP scores when you have taken an AP class, you can receive credit, placement or both? Your AP scores can earn you college credit or "advanced placement," which means you can move on to a more advanced course.

Build on Your Credentials

Hopefully, you've had the opportunity to explore extracurriculars in freshman year. Whether student government, Spanish club, investment club, mock trial, Model UN or any other activity, now's the time to focus on those you are excited about and take your involvement to the next level.

NARROW DOWN YOUR FOCUS AND DIVE DEEPER INTO YOUR EXTRACURRICULAR ACTIVITIES

You tried a variety of activities during freshman year. As a sophomore, focus in and spend more time on the ones that are most meaningful to you. Your extracurriculars will help you define who you are to the colleges to which you apply.

You are going to be asked to list them all on your applications and you don't want to find yourself with a blank page.

☑ TRY SOMETHING NEW

If you haven't found an activity that sparks your interest, try a new one. It's still early enough in high school to find extracurriculars outside of the classroom to get involved in. Make a list of the things you're drawn to and try to identify clubs or volunteer opportunities that match up. Take another look at the list of activities your school has to offer. Talk to your friends and ask about the clubs they're enjoying to get some ideas.

☑ DO YOU WANT TO START A NEW CLUB?

If, after speaking with your counselor and attending your school's activities fair, you still haven't found a club that matches your interests, consider starting a new one. Before you commit, make sure you have the time to devote to running a club. Talk to your classmates to find out if anyone else is interested. Follow through on your idea by registering with your school, planning the first meeting and getting the word out.

☑ CONNECT YOUR INTERESTS

If you have homed in on a few activities that you're excited about, now's the time to engage further and dedicate more time. If you're currently involved in an in-school activity, explore ways to expand your involvement by engaging with your local community. For example, if you're a peer tutor in school, you may want to volunteer at the local Boys & Girls Club as an after-school homework helper. Further developing your interests may also lead you to an area of study in college as well as a potential career path.

 ## DECIDE HOW TO BEST EXPAND YOUR INVOLVEMENT

Think ahead about how you can grow from a member in tenth grade to a leader in eleventh or twelfth grade. Leadership skills are great life skills to develop and they are definitely among the ones that colleges are interested in seeing.

 ## CONSIDER VOLUNTEERING

Give back by committing some time to a local charity and become more involved in your community. Not only will this be a very rewarding experience, your time spent volunteering may help you fulfill your school's community service requirements too.

Be Organized

Although you're not ready to apply to college just yet, you can start preparing by setting up an organizing system specifically for your college process. Organization is the most effective tool to help you submit successful applications and present your best self to admissions representatives when the time comes. Once you begin your applications, you'll want to be ready for the barrage of requirements and deadlines. Set up an organizing system that works for you; whether it's a paper file or a folder on your computer, find the best storage system to save your documents.

✓ **Use a master list** to keep track of all the usernames and passwords required throughout the college process. Include your social security number on this list as well. You will be asked to create separate sign-ins for college and testing sites, as well as scholarship and financial aid applications, and you won't want to waste time looking up this information repeatedly. Staying organized and having easy access to what you need will save you lots of time and frustration throughout the process.

✓ **Keep a list** of dates, registration deadlines and locations for the standardized tests you schedule. Also, create another list for your test scores.

✓ **Keep track** of your involvement in activities outside of the classroom. List clubs, athletics and competitions with the dates you participated and any special accomplishments or positions. Continue to update this information throughout high school.

✓ **Keep a folder of work you're proud of.** When you apply to college, you may be asked to provide samples of your writing or research papers. Start building your portfolio now.

✓ **Organize your documents.** Save award certificates, standardized test score reports and transcripts all in one place so you can find them when you need them.

66

I should have kept my SAT score reports in a folder on my desk. If I had, I would have avoided my last-minute panic when the College Board's site was down and I needed my most recent scores to submit with my applications.

—Sasha A.   99

Plan Ahead

Sophomore year is like the calm before the storm. Junior year is a very important year in the college process and as a result will be very demanding. So in addition to staying on course this year, planning ahead will get you off to a solid start next year. It's a good idea to meet with your guidance counselor at least twice to map out your college process.

IN THE FALL

- Meet at the beginning of the school year to talk about and address how you're doing so far, both academically and personally.

- Start a conversation about standardized testing. Learn about the ACT vs. the SAT.

IN THE SPRING

Meet again in the spring semester to choose your junior year classes. Your counselor can also help you determine if opting into any honors and AP classes or the IB program is appropriate for you, if they are available at your school and you're eligible.

After taking practice tests and reviewing your PSAT scores, decide which test, if any, you'll be taking. Talk about how to prepare, and then work out when you'll take the tests.

Discuss options for your summer break. Work, take a college or university class either in an academic or nonacademic subject, or volunteer with an organization that has meaning to you. Summer is a great time to expand on the interests you've developed during the school year. What you choose to do with your time is a reflection of what's important to you. Keep in mind that colleges will want to know what you did each summer.

And while we're on the subject of planning ahead...

Did you know that your social media presence may play an important role in your college admissions process? Admissions officers look at applicants' social media to learn more about them, so think ahead next time you're getting ready to tweet or post a photo. What you put on the internet is there for good.

Try This

☺ Do something in the summer that you can build on in the coming school year and during the next summer as well. Commit to something and stick with it.

☺ Make the most of high school. You won't get a second chance. There are no do-overs.

☺ Test out your leadership skills and develop them further, whether for a club, your team, or even a class group project.

☺ Don't forget to read. Reading can be fun and improves your vocabulary.

Goals

- ☐ _____
- ☐ _____
- ☐ _____
- ☐ _____
- ☐ _____
- ☐ _____
- ☐ _____
- ☐ _____
- ☐ _____
- ☐ _____
- ☐ _____
- ☐ _____
- ☐ _____
- ☐ _____

☐ _____

☐ _____

☐ _____

☐ _____

☐ _____

☐ _____

☐ _____

☐ _____

☐ _____

☐ _____

☐ _____

☐ _____

☐ _____

☐ _____

☐ _____

☐ _____

Notes

CHAPTER 3

JUNIOR YEAR: CONTROL THE CHAOS

A lot goes on in junior year and you'll be very busy now that college is within reach. Your days are going to be filled with test prep, testing, college fairs, school research and campus tours, all while continuing to be immersed in academics, athletics, extracurriculars, work and family responsibilities. Now, exhale!

You're going to have a lot going on at the same time and so many things to keep track of and oversee. Manage all your responsibilities by staying organized. Do you have a system that's working for you? If so, keep using it. If not, now is the time to set one up to help you to keep it together and manage your time. Make a list of all your responsibilities and obligations. Prioritize your tasks and set a timeline. Make sure you're using a calendar to keep track of schoolwork deadlines, test registration deadlines and test dates, college fairs, appointments with your guidance counselor, college visits and any other commitments.

This will probably be your most important school year. Your grades throughout high school are indicators of not only your academic performance, but also your growth. If you had a slow start in ninth and tenth grades, you can show colleges your potential by improving now. Work hard to do well. If you're having difficulty, ask your teacher(s) for extra help before or after school. Organize a study group with classmates to help you keep up. Remember, junior year grades will be the last full year grades available for Admissions to review, so stay focused on your schoolwork.

Try to keep your stress level in check. While talk of the college process will be everywhere during junior year, don't let it consume you. Your neighbor, your great uncle, and your dentist, while all meaning well, will ask you where you're planning to go to college. Find something else to talk about with your friends and family, make time to do what you enjoy and take some time for yourself.

Keep in mind, there are many people who can offer you the support you need: your guidance counselor, a teacher or coach, a mentor or family friend, and of course, your family. All you need to do is ask for help.

66

I only realized how many things I had to juggle when I finished entering everything into my calendar. I couldn't believe it!

—Will T.   99

GAME PLAN

Who Are You

More About
Standardized Tests

Finding the
Right School

Jump Start Your
Applications

What Are You Going
To Do This Summer

Who Are You?

Criteria for college admissions include your academic performance, the degree of rigor of your coursework, standardized test scores if applicable, extracurricular involvement, recommendations and essays. You'll need to show that your interests connect, from course selection to after-school activities, both at school and in your community.

The schools you apply to will want to know more about you and what you've done in high school. Who will you present to college admissions? Are you an athlete? Artist? Science nerd? It's important to connect your activities and interests to create a personal profile that reflects your personality. Your essay will be your opportunity to tell admissions reps who you are. You'll want to connect your extracurricular activities, your community involvement and other responsibilities. By making that connection, you'll convey what is important to you and what you've chosen to prioritize. Maybe what you've been involved in throughout high school gives you an obvious common thread that helps you tell your story. On the other hand, if you haven't had one clear focus throughout high school so far, the good news is you still have time to identify and pursue activities that are meaningful to you and that will help you define yourself to Admissions. So find something new to get involved with through senior year or continue to build on what you've done so far.

Students with very specific interests may be required or may choose to submit supplemental material with their applications. If that's you, get started during this school year to lighten the demands on your time next year.

Tip: If you're a student athlete, talk to your coach about playing in college. Review eligibility requirements with your guidance counselor to make sure you have completed the needed coursework. Sign up online at the NCAA Eligibility Center. The NCAA recommends that student athletes register at the beginning of their junior year in high school. Athletes often provide videos to college recruiters, so if that's something you have in mind, make sure to take care of it during this year's playing season.

Tip: As a musician or another kind of performing artist, you may be asked to submit samples of your work. Some schools require a video recording prior to an audition and have very specific instructions and requirements for this performance. Be sure to confirm what will be needed.

Tip: As a fine artist, you may be asked to submit a portfolio with your application. Students hoping to attend fine arts programs in college should use this time to put together a body of work appropriate to include in a portfolio. Find information online about National Portfolio Day, which offers an opportunity to have your work critiqued by professional representatives of accredited colleges and universities.

Tip: If scientific research has been your focus, you may want to consider submitting a supplement to your applications. This would include a complete list of the competitions you have participated in, including the title of your research projects, your placement in each event, and any abstracts and other publications of your work. Put this together during junior year so you have it ready to go with your applications next fall.

More About Standardized Tests

To test or not to test? Every college and university has its own testing requirements. In recent years, more and more schools have shifted to a test optional admissions policy. The 2020 coronavirus pandemic significantly disrupted college admissions and accelerated that movement. Now, there is a wider range of schools that are test optional, meaning they do not require students to submit test scores when applying. As some students test very well and others have difficulty with standardized testing, this is a personal decision. Test scores are just one component of the application. Do you have strong grades, a deep commitment to your activity(s), a unique skill or talent, a special story? Consider who you will be presenting to Admissions for evaluation. As you'll want to submit the strongest application possible, include your test scores if they'll add value to your candidacy.

At the beginning of this year, chances are you don't yet know where you'll be applying to college, nor do you know how strong your test results will be. Keep your options open by opting in to standardized testing unless you have a compelling reason to do otherwise.

 ## REGISTER FOR THE PSAT IN SEPTEMBER

If you want to qualify for the National Merit Scholarship, you need to take the PSAT in junior year.

 ## TAKE PRACTICE TESTS TO HELP DECIDE WHICH TEST TO FOCUS ON

Both ACT and College Board offer free online tests. It's a good idea to review the results with your guidance counselor to identify the best exam for you.

 ## MAKE A PLAN

Develop your own personal testing schedule. Look at the test dates available online and decide which dates work best with your academic calendar and allow you enough time to prepare. Once you've figured all that out:

✓ Register early to secure a spot at the test center of
your choice.

✓ Consider the test preparation choices available to you.
Prepare either on your own using review books and
online programs, with the help of a private tutor, or in
a group class at your local library, community center or
with any test prep service. Do your research and ask your
guidance counselor, teachers, friends and classmates
for recommendations.

✓ Sign up online for the SAT Question of the Day and ACT
Question of the Day to help you practice.

✓ Evaluate your test results. If you're not satisfied and feel
you have room for improvement, consider preparing
further and retaking the test. It's not uncommon for
students to take a test more than once.

✓ If you're enrolled in AP classes, make sure to sign up for
the AP exams. Talk to your teacher for details on how to
register and how best to prepare. Make the most of teacher
review sessions, peer study groups and online resources.

☑ GET READY FOR TEST DAY

✓ Arrange how you'll get to the test center.

✓ Pack the required items, including:
   Test admissions ticket, photo ID, two No. 2 pencils with
   erasers, an approved calculator.

✓ Also, bring any of these additional items:
   A watch, backup calculator, extra batteries, a drink
   and a snack.

Finding the Right School

Statistics for students who have gained admission are available on college and university websites. You can find data on high school course prerequisites, GPAs and test scores to give you an idea of what you need to qualify for admission. A school that's right for you should match your interests, abilities and needs. Start with an open mind as you explore your options.

I thought I was the perfect candidate because my SAT scores and GPA were inside the ranges I'd read about online. My guidance counselor explained being at the low end of the range was no guarantee of acceptance.

—Dan C.

Your counselor knows you, your high school and the college landscape, and can help you develop a preliminary list of schools to research.

Based on your interests, academic performance, test results and the admissions outcomes for students who graduated from your school before you, your counselor can help you narrow down your choices.

USE THESE RESOURCES TO HELP YOU WITH YOUR RESEARCH:

College guidebooks including *Fiske Guide to Colleges*, *Princeton Review* and *Barron's* provide a general overview of a school's offerings and stats.

College and university websites offer virtual tours and information about schools.

College admissions blogs will catch you up on the latest news and topics in the college admissions world.

Online systems your school uses, such as Naviance, have search tools that provide information specific to students applying from your high school.

Net Price Calculator, the US Department of Education's online tool, which is available on every school's website, will help you understand the real price of attending college.

I learned about the most recent schools to adopt test optional policies by reading the education section of the newspaper.

—David P.

ATTEND COLLEGE FAIRS

College fairs are a great way to get acquainted with many colleges and universities in one place. You can learn more about the schools you're interested in, get introduced to schools with which you may not be familiar and connect with admissions reps.

✓ Find out about fairs in your area, both in-person and virtual. The best place to start is with your guidance counselor. Look online for the National Association for College Admission Counseling's schedule of fairs at nacacfairs.org. Also, check virtualcollegefairs.org for a list of fairs to attend.

✓ Prepare in advance by reviewing the list of participating schools and deciding which reps you'd like to meet and which events you'd like to attend, then plan your day.

VISIT A CAMPUS

Campus visits are the best way to learn about different types of schools and get an up-close look at what really goes on at a college. If you're not able to travel far, visit schools close to home. Most schools offer both tours, which are usually led by students, and info sessions, which are typically conducted by members of Admissions both on campus and virtually. Reserve your spot in advance if required.

- Take a tour. Tours give you the opportunity to look at what the campus facilities have to offer and give you a chance to see the school through a current student's eyes and ask questions.

- Sign up for an information session. Info sessions are a way to learn about the school from Admissions staff, who will make a formal presentation followed by a Q & A session. Feel free to ask questions, but focus on asking those that can't be answered on the school's website.

- If you have the chance to visit a campus, spend time after the tour and info session exploring. Eat in the cafeteria, visit the student center, try to sit in on a class. Talk with current students, read the school newspaper and check out the bulletin boards around campus. Ask students you meet the questions you really want the answers to but don't want to ask on a tour or during the info session.

I was so glad I had prepared some questions for the
tour guide. She was so helpful and really gave me
honest answers.

—Melanie S.

MEET WITH COLLEGE REPS WHEN THEY VISIT YOUR HIGH SCHOOL

These sessions offer an opportunity for you to learn
more and get a feel for the school's personality to
start a conversation and make a connection.

- Sign up for the event, if required.

- Prepare questions in advance to ask the rep. Again, make
  sure you have questions that cannot be answered by
  reading through the school website.

- Follow up with an email or phone call to ask additional
  questions, or thank the rep for their time and to
  demonstrate your interest.

And while we're on the subject of demonstrating your interest...

Did you know that many, although not all, schools keep track of a student's demonstrated interest?

Show you're interested by signing up for the school's mailing list, meeting with reps when they visit your high school, reaching out and sending an email to ask questions. Also, attend a campus tour and/ or information session, either on campus or online, participate in an admissions event in your area and request an alumni interview.

Some schools even track how quickly their emails are opened by prospective students.

 # REMEMBER THE DETAILS

Whether a tour is in person or virtual, there's so much to take in. This may be the first time you're either on a campus or taking a close look, and it can be both exciting and overwhelming.

After a while, it's hard to recall the details of one campus
from another: which one had the up-to-date athletic center,
which cafeteria had great food choices and which dorms
were the newest. Try the following to help you remember:

✓ Take notes about what you see.

✓ Be aware of how you feel. Can you see yourself as a part of
   this campus community for the next four years?

✓ Use photos to remind yourself of what you saw.

✓ Jot down reminders about any meaningful conversations
   and collect business cards or contact info to follow up.

Jump-Start Your Applications

➤ OPEN YOUR COMMON APPLICATION ACCOUNT

The Common App is an undergraduate application accepted by over eight hundred colleges and universities. There's a good chance the schools you'll be applying to will require you to complete this application.

Fact: You can create a Common App account at any time.

Fact: Your account rolls over from year-to-year using the same password.

Fact: The Common App allows you to apply to multiple colleges at once.

Fact: Specifics regarding individual school requirements are available on the Common App.

Fact: You can get a look at the required essay topics ahead of time so you can start brainstorming.

Fact: You don't have to complete the application in one sitting—work at your own pace, saving your work as you go along.

Fact: You can monitor the progress of your applications in the Common App portal.

➤ REQUEST RECOMMENDATIONS

Most colleges require two letters of recommendation, usually from your primary subject teachers in junior or senior year. Your counselor can help you decide which teachers to ask for recommendations.

Tip: If possible, request recommendations in person. Many teachers receive more requests than they can possibly write, so asking in person and in advance increases the chances of making it on to their list. We suggest taking care of this in the spring of junior year to give your teachers enough notice.

Tip: If you have been seriously involved in a program such as science research or athletics, you may also consider including a letter from a teacher or coach who knows you well.

Tip: We suggest providing teachers with information that will help them write the most effective letters, including an outline highlighting the time you've spent in their classroom, listing some favorite assignments and samples of your work. Also, you can let them know what you enjoyed most about their class and share any experiences outside the classroom that are relevant to their subject matter.

Tip: If you have a résumé, you should share that with your recommenders as well. Providing this information will help them write the best possible letter tying together all your related experiences.

My Top Picks for Recommenders

➤ SORT THROUGH YOUR SAVED SCHOOLWORK

Your graded schoolwork can play a very important role in
your college application process and even after college. Saving
the high school papers that you're most proud of is a good
idea because there are many occasions when you may be
asked to submit a writing sample. Keep your work organized
now to have it accessible when you need it. Until you have
college level work to submit, you'll want to know where to
find your best high school papers. Keep in mind the following
points before you clean out that desk drawer of yours.

Fact: Many test optional schools request or require a graded
assignment from high school.

Fact: When applying to a specific program, whether as a high
school senior or as an enrolled student, samples of your work may
be required.

Fact: Many internship and work opportunities also request a
writing sample.

What Are You Going to Do This Summer?

When we think of summer, we think about fun in the sun: hanging out at the beach, swimming at the local pool with friends and barbecues. Regardless of what you decide to do, also look to build new skills or deepen ones you already have. Be productive and get things done that have been on your "to-do" and "try this" lists. Challenge yourself to learn something new. Remember, admissions reps will want to see how you spent your time in and out of the classroom all year long.

Tip: Put together a new résumé or update your current one to highlight all the activities you've been involved with in and out of school during your high school years. You can easily find a template online to get started. Include personal and academic information, extracurricular activities, athletic participation, work experiences, volunteer commitments and special skills. Make sure to note the dates of your participation, emphasize any leadership positions, and list awards and achievements. Your résumé will be helpful to your guidance counselor and teachers when writing letters of recommendation for your college admissions applications. If you're looking for a job or internship, you'll be all ready to apply.

Tip: Consider taking a college course either on a campus or online to give you a taste of college level work. This is also a great way to further an academic interest.

Tip: Continue your involvement and deepen your commitment to your interests, activities, work or volunteer obligations, and/or athletic participation.

Tip: Review the list of schools that interest you.

- Look at their websites and know what is needed to apply.
- Plan any virtual or in-person school visits you'd like to make over the summer. Remember to reserve your spot for info sessions and tours, if required.

Tip: Get organized. In addition to your commitments, as a rising senior, this summer is a very important time to focus on your college application process. Once senior year begins, you'll be busy keeping up with all your responsibilities both in and out of school. Here are some things to get started on:

- If you've opted in to standardized testing, decide whether you're satisfied with your score(s).

- Register for any additional test(s) you may want to take and continue with test prep.

- If you have not already done so, open a Common App account and work on your application.

  o   Fill in all the personal information first.

  o   Complete the activities section by using the log you've been keeping since freshman year. List your activities in order of importance to you.

  o   Look through the essay prompts and start brainstorming ideas, then begin writing your essay. Decide what you'll want to say and think about how you will tell your story.

- If you've narrowed down your list of schools, get a jump start on any supplemental essays required. Regarding those "optional" essays, they're not optional!

And while we're on the subject of college essays...

Did you know that your essay is how you'll tell admissions reps who you really are, what you have to offer and what you'll bring to their campus? Even a topic that's ordinary and everyday can help tell your unique story if you do it in a thoughtful way. It's not the topic, but how you relate that topic to your life circumstances that's important. Weave your interests together with your experiences and tell your personal tale with authenticity and passion. Highlight who you are, what you've done and what your goals are to demonstrate your qualities and individuality for Admissions to see.

Try This

☺ Start test prep early so you can be ready to take the tests and be done with them in junior year, if possible.

☺ Research and find three schools your classmates are not considering.

☺ Become a regular visitor to the guidance office, get comfortable with their resources and get to know the staff.

Goals

- [ ] _____
- [ ] _____
- [ ] _____
- [ ] _____
- [ ] _____
- [ ] _____
- [ ] _____
- [ ] _____
- [ ] _____
- [ ] _____
- [ ] _____
- [ ] _____
- [ ] _____
- [ ] _____

- [ ] _____
- [ ] _____
- [ ] _____
- [ ] _____
- [ ] _____
- [ ] _____
- [ ] _____
- [ ] _____
- [ ] _____
- [ ] _____
- [ ] _____
- [ ] _____
- [ ] _____
- [ ] _____
- [ ] _____
- [ ] _____

Notes

SENIOR YEAR: YOU'RE ALMOST THERE

Senior year will very likely be your most memorable year in high school. You know your teachers and principal, and have probably shared classes and activities with the same group for several years now. You're comfortable in your surroundings and it's your turn to rule the school. You have so much to look forward to, from being a part of special senior student days and events to graduation festivities and everything in between, including submitting your applications, receiving acceptance letters and deciding where to go to college. Before you get to all the fun stuff and close this chapter, you have some important work to do.

This is the final leg of your journey to college. Finish strong and don't let anything disrupt your college bound plans. Stay focused on your schoolwork—admissions officers will consider your mid-year grades when they review your applications. Continue to show up and stay committed to your extracurriculars because people are counting on you.

In addition to your schoolwork and activities, you should also be preparing for any additional tests, researching schools and planning visits, scheduling interviews, writing your essays and working on your college applications. Until you've completed and submitted all your applications, you're going to be extremely busy. So don't put things off, get started now.

66

I didn't realize how many deadlines I would be
keeping track of. Even within the same school there
were different deadlines.

—Jacinda V.   99

It's natural to feel stressed and overwhelmed by all the demands
on your time. You may find that everyone around you is
consumed by the college process and only talking about that;
try not to get caught up in the buzz. Keep things in the proper
perspective. You're going to find more than one school that
can be a great fit for you. Take a fresh look and see if there are
any additional schools to research. From the thousands of
colleges and universities to choose from there are many where
you can thrive academically, socially and personally. Who you
are is not defined by the name of the college or university you
attend. What is important is what you choose to engage with in
the school community and the relationships you develop with
faculty and classmates.

Don't be shy about reaching out to your support system. Be
proactive. Make an appointment with your guidance counselor
and talk with your teachers, school administrators, coaches and
assistant principals. Reach out to college admission officers
with questions specific to their school as well as admissions
requirements and policies—this is the time to make a
connection and show them you're interested.

VOCABULARY WORDS

ABOUT DEADLINES

EARLY ACTION (EA) allows a student to demonstrate their interest in being admitted to a school without having to make a binding commitment. EA policies vary from school to school. Restrictive EA schools do not allow applicants to apply EA or ED to other schools, while nonrestrictive EA schools permit students to submit EA or ED applications elsewhere. Applications are due early to mid-November and decisions are released by mid-December.

EARLY DECISION (ED), offered by some schools, is binding, so applicants should be sure that this is the right school for them. Application deadlines are early to mid-November and decisions are released in mid-December. Only one ED application may be submitted.

EARLY DECISION II (EDII) is also offered by only a limited number of schools. Students can choose one school to apply as an EDII applicant and acceptance is binding. Application deadlines are around January 1 and decisions are released in mid-February.

OPEN ENROLLMENT schools accept applicants regardless of grades and consider applications until all spaces for the incoming class are full.

REGULAR DECISION deadlines vary from school to school. Typically, applications are due between January 1 and mid-February. Decisions are usually sent out between mid-March and early April.

ROLLING ADMISSIONS applications are reviewed by schools as they are received, so applying early may improve odds of acceptance. Decisions are released as application are processed.

ABOUT THE AID APPLICATIONS

CSS/PROFILE is an application that must be submitted to help schools determine eligibility for non-federal student aid.

FAFSA (Free Application for Federal Student Aid) is an application for federal and state aid programs. The application opens October 1 each year and can be completed at fafsa.ed.gov.

SAR (Student Aid Report) summarizes the information submitted on the FAFSA and will include a Student Aid Index. Upon receipt, within four weeks, the student is responsible for confirming the accuracy of the information on the report and making any necessary corrections.

STUDENT AID INDEX (formerly known as the Expected Family Contribution) is an index number that colleges use to determine how much a family can afford to pay for college. The Student Aid Index can be found on the SAR.

ABOUT THE DIFFERENT TYPES OF AID

GRANTS/SCHOLARSHIPS are often called gift aid because they are almost always tax-free and do not have to be repaid.

LOANS are funds from the government, colleges, or others that must be repaid, each comes with its own repayment schedule and interest rate.

MERIT-BASED AID is awarded without regard to a family's need.

NEED-BASED AID is awarded based on a family's finances.

NON-SUBSIDIZED LOANS are not based on need. Although the interest accrues from the start of school, the student has the option to pay interest while in school or defer paying interest on such loans until after graduation and repay along with the principal.

PELL grants are need-based federal grants that do not have to be repaid.

PLUS LOANS are fixed rate loans issued by the US Department of Education, available to parents of undergraduate students to help pay for college expenses not covered by other forms of financial aid.

PRIVATE LOANS are available from a variety of lenders, financial institutions, private organizations and nonprofits, and have varying terms.

SCHOOL GRANTS may be need or merit based.

SCHOOL LOANS are made by the college or university. Requirements and availability can be confirmed with the financial aid office.

STATE GRANTS are based on need and come with residency requirements for eligibility.

STATE LOAN PROGRAMS, available to state residents, are not need-based. Repayment options vary and may include deferments until after graduation, flexible repayment options based on income, loan forgiveness for public service and deferment for financial hardship.

SUBSIDIZED LOANS are need-based loans with interest that does not accrue while the student is in school.

TUITION WAIVERS are granted by colleges to eligible students including dependents of eligible employees, teaching assistants, resident advisors, state employees and members of the military.

WORK-STUDY PROGRAMS are the part of the financial aid package that offers students part-time jobs, usually on campus.

GAME PLAN

Meet with Your
Guidance Counselor

More About
Standardized Tests

Submitting Your
Applications

Paying for College

The Home Stretch

Meet with Your Guidance Counselor

Schedule a meeting with your counselor as soon as you're back from summer break. Although it may seem you have plenty of time, college applications will be due before you know it.

- ✓ **Review your scores and goals with your counselor** to determine which if any tests you'll take and then register for your preferred testing date(s).

- ✓ **Confirm each school's deadlines for receiving test scores** in order for them to be considered. Make sure the testing service is able to send your scores by that date.

- ✓ **Ask your guidance counselor if you qualify for fee waivers** from the College Board and/or ACT.

✓ **Narrow down your list.** Your goal is to have a balanced list of about ten schools that are a mix of safety schools, target schools and reach schools, both academically and financially.

✓ **Ask for input on whether to apply early decision (ED) or early action (EA).** Discuss your chance of admission and get advice as to whether applying early is right for you. Your counselor knows how students from your school have fared with admissions at particular schools in the past. They also know if other students from your class are considering the same schools.

✓ **Get ready for the November deadline** if you're going to apply as an ED or EA applicant.

✓ **Discuss your need for financial aid and ask for help completing required forms**, including the FAFSA, CSS/Profile and any state and school specific applications.

✓ **Find out about scholarship opportunities.** Your counselor can be helpful in searching for scholarships and nominating you for grants and special programs.

✓ **Help your counselor write an effective letter of recommendation on your behalf.** Share your résumé and complete any counselor questionnaires they may have. Make sure your guidance counselor knows which schools you are most interested in and understands why.

Where Will You Apply?

College is finally within sight. You did all the work to get here and now you have some big decisions to make. Where will you apply? Will you submit applications for early decision or early action? If so, where? One reason to consider an early application is that admission rates for early applicants are generally higher than for those who apply regular decision. However, if you require financial aid to attend college and would like the opportunity to compare aid packages from the schools that accept you, then early decision may not be right for you. Here's your next checklist:

✓ **Review your list of schools with your family** to make sure you're all comfortable with your choices. Chances are it's still a work in progress. Since your last discussion, things may have changed; you may have a better test score, your family's

financial situation may be altered or your comfort level with
distance from home may be different.

✓ **Work on creating a balanced list of safety, target and reach
schools.** Academic safety schools include those where your
grades and test scores are in the upper end of the ranges of
students who were accepted in the past, particularly from your
high school. Academic target schools are those where your
grades and scores are in the mid-ranges of accepted students.
Academic reach schools are schools that mostly accept students
whose credentials are generally higher than yours.

✓ **Finalize your list,** keeping in mind that good outcomes are
based on a good list. Your best possible outcomes will result
from identifying schools that are looking for students with your
profile. Objective admissions criteria are grades, test scores,
and demographics, while subjective factors include special
interests, talents and achievements or your special story, any
of which make you unique. The process is full of uncertainty
as admissions criteria shift from year to year, so make sure
that you would be happy to attend each and every college on
your list.

✓ **Decide whether you're going forward with early decision
or early action.** In addition to your early school, maintain
a list of schools you plan to apply to if your early outcome
doesn't work out.

I made a chart and filled in the schools I was applying to. I also added to the chart all the application and aid deadlines. Then, I checked each box as I submitted my applications. This system definitely helped me stay on time and keep track of everything.

—Katie R.

Submitting Your Applications

Now that you have a list of schools, you can start submitting applications. Give yourself enough time, pay attention to the details and don't let the mechanics trip you up. Meeting deadlines, checking for spelling errors and typos, and making sure you're sending in all the required components are some of the things you have to manage. You are also responsible for requesting and making sure that your standardized test scores and letters of recommendation are submitted on time.

✓ **Find your list of usernames and passwords.** You'll need this information repeatedly now that you're ready to apply. Don't waste time trying to retrieve forgotten passwords.

✓ **Create a chart that includes each of your schools and their deadlines.** Applications, special programs, financial aid forms and scholarships all have distinct due dates, and these dates are final. Deadlines may vary from one school to another and even within schools for different programs. No matter how qualified you may be, a missed deadline is a missed opportunity.

✓ **Create a Common App account** if you haven't already done so, and look into the Coalition Application and the Universal College Application, if required by any of the schools on your list.

✓ **Open an online account with colleges and universities that do not use the Common App but have their own applications.** Don't forget to save these usernames and passwords on your master list as well.

✓ **Continue working on the other applications on your list** in case you don't receive good news regarding your ED or EA application(s).

✓ **Be sure to confirm submission details for supplementary materials** if the program to which you are applying requests or requires you to do so.

✓ **Get into the habit of backing up your work** to save the many documents you'll be creating throughout the time you're working on your applications.

✓ **Proofread your essays.** They should be well-written and in your own voice. Make sure you have no typos or spelling mistakes. It's okay to seek out help from a proofreader, but make sure your essays are in your own words. Admissions officers want

to hear what you have to say, not your parent or teacher
or mentor.

66

*I saved myself a lot of work and used one essay for
all my applications. I made a huge mistake, though,
when I copied and pasted the essay and didn't
change the name of the school I was talking about.*

—Josh E.   99

✓ **Confirm with your recommenders** that they'll be writing on
your behalf and provide them with your final list of schools.

✓ **Request the College Board or ACT send your test scores to
the schools on your list.** Ask your guidance counselor for fee
waiver information if needed.

✓ **Schedule your admissions interviews.** As soon as you've
submitted any one component of your application, a school
creates your admissions file. At this point, you can request an
interview. Openings are often limited, so don't wait.

✓ **Schedule alumni interviews.** Even if interviews are not
required, take the opportunity to connect with an alum and
learn more about the school and share why you'd like to attend.
Check the website to confirm who is responsible for scheduling
your interview.

✓ **Get ready for your interviews.** Research the school carefully, prepare questions and responses to potential questions, and practice with a family member or friend.

✓ **Proofread your applications thoroughly, several times.** Ask a family member or friend to double-check that your application is in order.

✓ **Pay the application fee or use a fee waiver, and then press submit.** Don't wait until the last minute because the systems can get overloaded with submissions and crash. You don't want to miss the deadline.

Paying for College

College is expensive, not only because of the high cost of tuition, but also due to the expenses required for books, student fees, lab fees, special events and everyday living expenses too. Financial aid money is available from a number of sources including the US federal government, the state where you live, the college you will attend and both nonprofit and private organizations. The more you understand about the system, the more successful you will be in gaining aid. Don't miss the opportunity to apply for financial aid; you won't know if you qualify unless you apply.

HOW TO APPLY FOR AID

Tip: Get an estimate of your cost to attend using the Net Price Calculator for each school on your list.

Tip: Compare cost to attend and average financial aid awards on the College Board's website at: bigfuture.com.

Tip: Check in with each individual school to determine what type of aid they offer and which forms they require.

Tip: Meet with your counselor for help on how and where to search for scholarships.

Tip: Use online tools such as bigfuture.com's Scholarship Search and fastweb.com to find scholarship opportunities.

Tip: Contact local and community organizations, employers, professional associations, and religious and cultural groups to which you are affiliated to ask about their scholarship opportunities.

Tip: Attend a financial aid workshop either online or at your school or local library to help you better understand how to complete the necessary forms.

Tip: Work on the FAFSA and CSS/Profile and any other financial aid forms, including scholarship applications. Make note of the opening dates and submit your applications as soon as possible, as aid is often awarded on a first-come-first-serve basis.

Tip: Review your Student Aid Report (SAR), which should arrive in your inbox after your FAFSA has been received. Respond promptly to any requests for information.

Tip: If you submitted the CSS/Profile and/or any state applications for aid, also be on the lookout for any requests for additional information.

And while we're on the subject of completing your FAFSA...

If you need support, some states run College Goal Sunday, a free program to help students and their families complete the FAFSA. Find details about this program online.

COMPLETE YOUR FAFSA

Tip: Check online for the FAFSA opening date and create FAFSA IDs for both yourself and your parents so that you can begin the application. It may take up to three days to get the IDs.

Tip: Work on and then submit your FAFSA as soon as possible, but no later than the due date. Note that deadlines vary from school to school.

Tip: Use the IRS retrieval tool link in the FAFSA to upload your family's tax information into the form.

Tip: Double-check that you've entered all the required information and that it's accurate because any mistakes or omissions may result in delays and missed aid opportunities.

Tip: Make sure you list all the colleges you're considering on your FAFSA because state aid applications use your FAFSA information as well. You don't need to have submitted a college application before listing the school on your FAFSA.

Tip: Find out whether your state requires you to list your schools on your FAFSA in a particular order. Check studentaid.gov for state- specific requirements. The order you choose to list your schools does not have any impact on federal aid.

Tip: Make sure you and your parents both electronically sign the FAFSA with your FAFSA IDs, and be certain you remember to submit it when complete.

Tip: Don't miss out on aid—you must complete a FAFSA to qualify for any type of aid, whether based on need or merit.

The Home Stretch

Although the hard work is behind you, the application process is not over just yet. College is within reach, so don't let anything stand in your way.

WHAT TO DO AFTER YOU'VE APPLIED

✓ Confirm that all the components of your application have been received. Your test scores, transcript, mid-year grades and recommendations are all coming from different sources. Check in the Common App or individual school portals or call each admissions office to make sure your file is complete.

✓ Share any new achievements with your admissions reps. Communicate only meaningful and significant accomplishments that enhance your applications. For example, if you have won an award or a contest or have had any of your work published, let them know.

✓ If you applied for early decision and have been accepted, congratulations! Accept the offer, share the news with your counselor, withdraw any other applications you submitted, and celebrate.

✓ If you were accepted ED and require financial aid, review your aid package and reach out to your financial aid rep if you have any questions or if the offer is not sufficient.

✓ If you applied EA and were accepted but want to wait for other outcomes, there's nothing further to do at this time.

✓ If you applied ED and were deferred and this is still your first choice school, then reach out to your admissions rep immediately to express interest in attending and ask your counselor to speak on your behalf as well. Make sure to submit your other applications by the due dates.

✓ Avoid senioritis. Your admission, financial aid, and scholarship offers are contingent on maintaining your academic standing, so stay on track.

✓ Check your emails daily. The schools to which you have applied may be reaching out with news or asking for more information.

HOW DO YOU DECIDE?

Seniors, this is the moment you've been waiting for after having worked so hard for four years and having survived the application process. You're probably sorting through acceptances, maybe rejections and perhaps even some waitlist or delayed acceptances.

Take a deep breath and review your options to make the choice that's best for you.

If you've received more than one acceptance:

✓ Look back on any notes you may have taken during your college search and reach out to any current students you know to hear more about their experiences.

✓ Try to remember how you felt while you were on campus, if you visited a school. Search through your notes and photos.

✓ Take a virtual tour of the schools you're considering.

✓ Meet your prospective classmates online.

✓ Sign up to attend admitted student programs.

✓ Make a pro/con list to help organize your thoughts and ask your parents for their feedback. Think about what's important to you, including price, financial aid, distance, programs, size and spirit, and compare each school to another.

✓ Ask your guidance counselor for their input and advice.

✓ Review your aid packages carefully. Make sure you understand the details.

✓ Reach out to financial aid officers for answers to any questions you have.

✓ Compare your financial aid packages to determine the best option for you. Note that aid information is not presented uniformly. Be clear about your offer—particularly what portion is made up of grants and what portion is made up of loans.

✓ Make sure you're comfortable with the amount that must be repaid and the terms of repayment.

✓ If the aid package is not enough, contact your financial aid rep to talk about your family's need and ask about the appeal process. This is your opportunity to negotiate the best possible package.

66

I received a generous offer from my second choice school. I'm so glad my counselor advised me to reach out to the financial aid officer at my top school to ask if they could match it. They did!

—Lindsay T.

99

✓ Submit your deposit with all the required documents and information by the due date, usually May 1, to reserve your spot in the incoming class. You cannot send a deposit to more than one school.

✓ Finally, decline any other offers of admission.

If you've been waitlisted, there's still a chance you may be admitted. While the admissions office may provide you with information about previous years' waitlists, the number of students admitted varies from year to year. There are seven things you should take care of as soon as possible:

✓ Send in the required response card to put yourself on the waitlist by the deadline, as soon as possible, as you will not be placed on the list automatically.

✓ Contact the school to ask whether aid will be available if you're admitted from the waitlist.

✓ Reach out to your admissions rep by phone or email to express your continued interest in being admitted and offer to provide any additional information in support of your candidacy.

✓ Update them about any new achievements not included in your file.

✓ If this is truly your top choice, let your admissions rep know that if you're admitted, you'll definitely attend.

✓ Talk to your guidance counselor and ask them to reach out to the school rep on your behalf.

✓ Waitlist decisions may arrive after deposits are due, so in the meantime, evaluate any other choices you may have and send in your deposit by the due date. Please note that deposits are nonrefundable. So if you're admitted from a waitlist and choose to attend that school, you'll forfeit the deposit you sent to the other school.

Some colleges offer delayed admission, but not until the second semester or even the following fall. If you are contemplating delayed admission, evaluate your options to decide what you'll do in the interim. Consider doing the following:

✓ Take classes at another college or university. Confirm first that your credits will be transferable to the school you're considering.

✓ Study abroad

✓ Volunteer

✓ Work

✓ Travel

WHAT IF YOU'RE NOT HAPPY?

If you're not happy with your choices, it's not too late to apply to schools with both rolling and late admissions deadlines.

✓ Check with your guidance office for a list of rolling admissions schools.

✓ Look online at NACAC's (National Association of College Admission Counseling) "College Openings Update," which

provides a list of over four hundred public and private
US colleges and universities with openings, financial
aid and housing available to qualified freshmen and/or
transfer students.

✓ Continue to look at the NACAC list because it is revised
as schools finalize their admissions numbers for the
upcoming year.

> " Although I was accepted to one of the schools on
> my original list, I realized how much my priorities
> had changed from the fall of senior year when I first
> made that list. By spring, I decided I was ready to go
> away to school. My guidance counselor suggested
> a few more schools that were still accepting
> applications in the spring.
>
> —Jordan M.   "

WRAPPING IT UP

Once you've made your big decision and sent in your deposit,
there are still a few more things to cross off your to-do list:

✓ Confirm that your high school transcript has been sent to the
school you'll be attending.

✓ Make sure you've accepted your financial aid package and completed any necessary paperwork.

✓ Save a copy of each of your applications.

✓ Save your test score reports.

✓ Save a copy of your final high school transcript.

✓ Save your résumé.

✓ Save important schoolwork.

66

I wasted so much time tracking down my SAT scores to submit with an internship application. I wish I had known to save my score reports.

—Kyle S.

99

Try This

☺ Find a scholarship with the most specific parameters that match up with who you are to increase your chances of being awarded funds.

☺ Thank all the people who have guided you through the process, either in person or by sending a note.

☺ Celebrate your first college acceptance letter.

Goals

- [ ] _____
- [ ] _____
- [ ] _____
- [ ] _____
- [ ] _____
- [ ] _____
- [ ] _____
- [ ] _____
- [ ] _____
- [ ] _____
- [ ] _____
- [ ] _____
- [ ] _____
- [ ] _____

- [ ] _____
- [ ] _____
- [ ] _____
- [ ] _____
- [ ] _____
- [ ] _____
- [ ] _____
- [ ] _____
- [ ] _____
- [ ] _____
- [ ] _____
- [ ] _____
- [ ] _____
- [ ] _____
- [ ] _____
- [ ] _____
- [ ] _____

Notes

CHAPTER 5

YOU'RE GOING TO COLLEGE: GET READY

Congratulations! You're on your way to college. This is a very exciting time, filled with new experiences, challenges and adjustments. Your college community is where you will be spending the majority of your time over the next four years. This is where you will attend classes, study, socialize and maybe even work. You will be meeting so many new people and making connections with classmates, professors, research partners, friends and mentors.

Get the most out of your college years. Be engaged by becoming involved. Find out what your school has to offer in the way of clubs, athletics, arts, special interest groups, volunteer opportunities and community service. Attend activity fairs so you can familiarize yourself with all the possibilities and then get involved. It's critical to find interests outside of the classroom, to connect and be part of campus life, to make the most of your college experience.

This may be your first time living away from home. Naturally, this can be both exciting and intimidating. Use the summer to prepare for this next step. Connect with your roommate and get to know one another. Whether you're going to be living on campus, off campus or commuting, be on the lookout for information about freshman orientation programs. Try to make every effort to attend, as these events are planned to help introduce you to the school and your future classmates before school begins. Everyone is just as eager to meet their peers and make friends.

Going to college is a big deal—for you, of course, but also for your family. Enjoy time with them and with your friends too.

This summer is the bridge between your high school and college years. Your high school was a familiar space and it will take time to settle into your new environment. Think about what worked for you in the past and what you'd like to change. This is an opportunity for a reset. College is all about making a new start—set yourself up for success.

GAME PLAN

First Steps

Next Steps

Register for Classes

Prepare to Live
on Campus

Choose Your Path

First Steps

You've made your decision, sent in your deposit and are now officially a member of your school community. Make sure to respond to any requests for information and complete all required forms by the given deadlines so that you don't miss out on any opportunities.

- ▶ Continue to check your email daily since your school will have lots of exciting news to share. Read everything your school sends you.

- ▶ Familiarize yourself with the academic calendar and take note of important dates, including dorm move-in and semester start and end dates.

- ▶ Research your tuition payment options. Some schools offer plans allowing you to spread out your payments.

- ▶ Fill out the housing forms and roommate questionnaires you've been sent if you're going to live on campus.

▶ Sign up for special orientation events. Many schools host programs for students and parents, together and/or separately.

▶ Complete all the necessary health insurance paperwork, or else opt out of your school's health insurance plan, if you're covered by your parents' policy. You will automatically be enrolled in the student health plan if you do not opt out, and you will be charged the insurance premium for that plan. So be mindful of the deadline.

▶ Schedule your physical, make sure you have the required immunizations, ask your doctor to complete all the required forms and submit them on time.

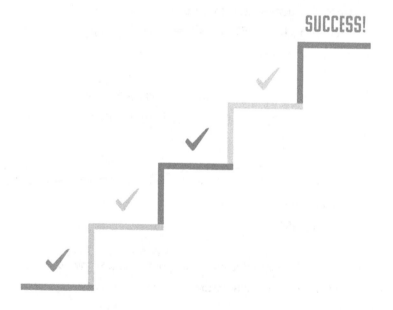

Next Steps

College life is going to offer you independence—most likely more than you had during high school. With that independence, you may find that you're tasked with new responsibilities. Start taking care of this to-do list during the summer before college begins.

- ▶ Go through your school's website with a new set of eyes to familiarize yourself with everything that will be available to you.

- ▶ Make a budget. Sit down with your parents, list your expenses and work out what they will be paying for and what you will be responsible for covering.

- ▶ If you've been awarded aid, reach out to your financial aid rep to establish a connection.

- ▶ If work-study is part of your financial aid package, ask how to apply for on and off-campus jobs and begin your search.

▶ Find out which computers your school recommends and
   supports. Explore your options—is there a special leasing or
   purchasing program for students?

▶ Verify that your computer and other valuables will be covered
   by your parents' homeowners insurance while you are
   at college.

▶ If you'll be driving to school, confirm whether you're
   covered by your parents' auto insurance. Also, look into the
   parking situation.

▶ Set up a bank account and apply for a credit and/or debit card.

▶ Complete any required reading you've been assigned for
   the summer.

Register for Classes

The number of courses offered at your college is most likely exponentially greater than what was available to you in high school. Going through the course catalog can be a daunting undertaking. Narrow down your choices by becoming familiar with the classes you will be required to take and then look into all the exciting new areas of study you can explore.

▶ Look through the course offerings and make sure you're aware of any first year requirements.

▸ If you took any AP exams in high school, confirm whether you'll receive credit or will place out of any entry-level courses.

▸ Learn more about your course options by looking through the online catalog thoroughly and carefully.

▸ Sign up for class times that are optimal for your own personal internal clock.

"

Signing up for an 8:00AM class was a mistake. I'm a late-night person and I should have known I wasn't going to ever get to class on time.

—Christopher G.   "

▸ When building your schedule, allow enough time between classes so you don't find yourself arriving late. Unlike in high school, your classrooms may be spread across the campus.

▸ Buy or lease your books once you've registered for your classes.

And while we're on the subject of choosing your classes...

Once you've found what you're interested in, dig through each class's syllabus so you know exactly what the instructor plans to cover. Look at the reading requirements, assignments and test schedules to make sure you know what you're signing up for.

Prepare to Live on Campus

For those of you going away to school, your campus will be your home away from home for the next four years. Pretty much everything you will need will be available on or near campus. With advanced planning, you can make this a smooth transition.

▷   Make sure you're aware of any pre-assigned move-in dates and times.

▶ Get to know your roommate. Depending on your school's policy, you may have had input on choosing your roommate or the school may have matched you up. Either way, don't be strangers on move-in day.

▶ Get ready for dorm life. Take inventory of what you already own and compare notes with your roommate to avoid duplication.

▶ If you're shopping for your dorm room, many stores provide helpful checklists and offer the option of selecting items locally and picking them up at the store closest to your school.

▶ Check out if your school offers any special packages for things like dorm room bedding and mini-refrigerator rentals, and find out about any restrictions or rules that may apply.

▶ If your family plans to stay in a hotel nearby, take care of reservations in advance since moving in often takes longer than expected and it will be a busy weekend on campus.

▶ Locate the nearest pharmacy and have your prescriptions transferred.

▶ When you pack, be sure to include personal health items like cold medicine, pain relievers, lozenges, etc.

▶ Learn how to do laundry. If you prefer to use the school's laundry service, complete the necessary paperwork to sign up.

▷ Acquire some basic cooking skills so you can make use of the
    hall kitchen for late nights, extra early mornings, or when you're
    just tired of the cafeteria food.

▷ Although it may seem too early, make hotel and restaurant
    reservations for homecoming weekend well in advance
    since it's one of the busiest weekends for the school and the
    surrounding community.

66

I attended a big university in a small town and my
family did not realize there were few hotels nearby.
We didn't think to make reservations far in advance
and unfortunately the only hotel that was available
was thirty minutes away.

—Lily A.   99

Choose Your Path

Keep in mind that what you do while you're in college is far more significant than where you attend. Of course academics are of paramount importance, but you should also make time to develop friendships, make connections and have new experiences

This is a time to figure things out. While some students know exactly what they want to study and have a clear career plan, most do not.

Try a variety of classes to find what sparks your interest. This is the right time for intellectual exploration.

Be open-minded about possible fields of study. Don't rush to decide on a major. Become informed by talking to upperclassmen, professors, people in the community, family members and family friends to learn more.

Get involved in campus life so you can get the most out of your college experience. Discovering what you're really interested in and excited by can help you define your future plans beyond college.

Make an effort to get to know your professors. Most have office hours where you can stop by or make an appointment. They can answer questions you may have or provide extra help with the course material.

Seek opportunities to assist a professor with their research or apply for a teaching assistant (TA) position.

Look into internship possibilities; internships can provide experiences that may help you decide on your career path.

And while we're on the subject of choosing your path...

Start networking by talking to like-minded people to exchange ideas, gather information and learn more about the world around you and opportunities for your future. Network to meet new people, build new relationships and make connections. Start with professors, your peers and local professionals and alumni who may be doing work you are interested to hear about, and may be offering mentoring and local or summer jobs.

Now that you've read through the book, consider where you are and where you want to go. Start thinking about how you'll get there and begin formulating your own personal plan to get yourself college ready.

Remember to be open-minded throughout high school. Take the opportunity to expose yourself to new ideas and experiences to learn more about what you may want to build into your future. As you grow and mature, your plans may change; and that's okay, because life is not a straight line and high school is all about figuring things out. If you encounter disappointments along the way, don't let them stop you. Regroup, make a new plan and move forward.

Be your best self by accepting your responsibilities and working hard. Becoming college ready is a process. It takes time to develop the academic skills you will need and the personal experiences that will help you to figure out what you care about and how you will choose to dedicate your time. Getting college ready is all within your control. Stay organized, focused and dedicated, and remain curious about the opportunities that will help you on your way to college.

Goals

- [ ] _____
- [ ] _____
- [ ] _____
- [ ] _____
- [ ] _____
- [ ] _____
- [ ] _____
- [ ] _____
- [ ] _____
- [ ] _____
- [ ] _____
- [ ] _____
- [ ] _____
- [ ] _____

☐ _____

☐ _____

☐ _____

☐ _____

☐ _____

☐ _____

☐ _____

☐ _____

☐ _____

☐ _____

☐ _____

☐ _____

☐ _____

☐ _____

☐ _____

☐ _____

☐ _____

Notes

_____

_____

_____

_____

_____

_____

_____

_____

_____

_____

_____

_____

_____

_____

ABOUT THE AUTHORS

Anna Costaras and **Gail Liss** are co-founders of Bound to Organize, LLC, an educational consulting firm.

Anna Costaras holds a BS and MBA from New York University Stern School of Business. A veteran of the college application process, Anna has counseled many students through their process and founded a college-bound mentoring program to provide guidance and support to undeserved students from her community. Anna has been actively involved with an educational enrichment program for children in need of after-school support. She has served as a volunteer, a college mentor and a member of the Board of Directors.

Gail Liss earned an MBA from New York University Stern School of Business, studied at The London School of Economics, and holds a BA from the University of Rochester. Gail serves on the Board of Trustees of an organization that delivers programming and services to residents across the five boroughs of New York City through dynamic community centers. Gail has extensive experience with the college application process and has served as a coach and advisor to college-bound students in a number of nonprofit organizations.

You can learn more about Anna and Gail, and Bound to Organize, LLC, by visiting: www.boundtoorganize.com

Mango Publishing, established in 2014, publishes an eclectic list of books by diverse authors—both new and established voices—on topics ranging from business, personal growth, women's empowerment, LGBTQ studies, health, and spirituality to history, popular culture, time management, decluttering, lifestyle, mental wellness, aging, and sustainable living. We were recently named 2019 *and* 2020's #1 fastest growing independent publisher by *Publishers Weekly*. Our success is driven by our main goal, which is to publish high quality books that will entertain readers as well as make a positive difference in their lives.

Our readers are our most important resource; we value your input, suggestions, and ideas. We'd love to hear from you—after all, we are publishing books for you!

Please stay in touch with us and follow us at:

Facebook: Mango Publishing
Twitter: @MangoPublishing
Instagram: @MangoPublishing
LinkedIn: Mango Publishing
Pinterest: Mango Publishing
Newsletter: mangopublishinggroup.com/newsletter

Join us on Mango's journey to reinvent publishing, one book at a time.

CPSIA information can be obtained
at www.ICGtesting.com
Printed in the USA
JSHW040344110721
16667JS00004B/18

9 781642 506044